CW01583395

To Love and To Cherish...

A Guide to the Marriage Service in
"The Alternative Service Book 1980"

John Mullett

Foreword by The Archbishop of York

CORTNEY PUBLICATIONS LUTON

Published in 1982

by

Cortney Publications Luton

ISBN 0 904378 16 0

Extracts from The Marriage Service in The Alternative Service Book 1980 are reproduced by permission of the Central Board of Finance of the Church of England; the complete text of the Service has not been included.

Cover Photograph by Ian Walters, Ashwell

Printed in Great Britain by
Inprint of Luton (Designers & Printers) Limited
95-115 Windmill Road, Luton, Bedfordshire, LU1 3XS   Telephone: (0582) 28161

CONTENTS

Foreword

by the Archbishop of York, Dr. Stuart Blanch

I am very happy to commend this guide book to those who are preparing for marriage. It could be a help to you also after your marriage. Some of the questions it raises will become real as a result of some experience of married life.

A happy home is a treasure beyond price, not only for yourselves but for your children and for all with whom you are associated. So treasure it! And persevere in it when the going is rough. Above all, learn to trust each other and to trust the God who made you.

May you be richly blessed in your life together.

Bishopthorpe, York ***Stuart Ebor***

Why Read this Guide?

Did you know how much you can now plan your Wedding Service in church and enjoy making it your very own? Never before has a couple who wished to be married in the Church of England had to make any substantial choices about the form of words used. In former times in our history when the Marriage Service has been revised, the old order was immediately declared to be null and void. Today this is not so. Church and Parliament have decreed that the couple concerned may choose if they wish to be married with the old 1662 Order of Service as printed in The Book of Common Prayer, or in its modified order called Series 1, or they may ask for the new order of the Marriage Service to be used as printed in "The Alternative Service Book 1980", (Pages 287–304)

The purpose of this guide book is to help you, the Bride and Groom, to make decisions, with your vicar, in three important matters.

(i) First of all you must decide whether or not you feel drawn towards the new order of service or the old.

(ii) If you prefer the new service then you must decide which of the two sets of vows you would wish to use.

(iii) Finally you must decide what the shape of your service will be; will it, for example, have readings from the scriptures before or after The Marriage; which prayers do you prefer and will the service include an opportunity for you to receive your Holy Communion?

In drafting the new service the revisers have purposely left much more scope for you the couple, to plan your service, and to make it your own. These pages are written to help you make your Wedding Day full of meaning and joy for you, your family and your guests.

The New Service and the Old Service

Most of us are conservative about religious things; we like the old hymns and the old texts of scripture which we know. If you were to read through the old service in "The Book of Common Prayer" and then immediately read through the service in "The Alternative Service Book 1980", what would you discover?

(i) **The similarities**

The vows in both services have very much the same ring about them and in fact the vows in The Book of Common Prayer are very similar indeed to those used in the Church of England as far back as the fourteenth century and earlier. When you come to Church, whichever service you use, you will be holding hands together and making solemn loving promises to each other in very much the same way, and in very much the same words, as Christian men and women have used for perhaps a thousand years. Just stop and think of all the various fashions of clothes that would have been worn for the services in that time! Meanwhile, the priest in the Church has gone on leading each couple, generation by generation, in very similar vows and prayers. 'Jesus Christ is the same yesterday today and forever' and his way of marriage is strong, secure and lasting.

If you want to be married with the old service and use words your parents may have used, don't be ashamed to ask for them. They are full of meaning.

(ii) **The differences**

You will find that in the introduction at the beginning of the old Marriage Service, people in ages past talked of the principles of marriage in ways that most of us would not use naturally today. Again, if you look at the prayers in the old order which come towards the end of the service you will find they are wordy and rather long. You must decide which is going to make your marriage something personal to you and most couples know quite quickly whether they are at home with the old words or the new.

The numbers in the margin correspond to the section numbers in 'The Alternative Service Book 1980" pages 287-304. Quotations from The Marriage Service are in heavy print. Quotations from scripture are taken from the N.E.B. or A.V. Translations.

A Journey Through the New Service

THE MARRIAGE

The bride and bridegroom stand before the priest, and the priest says

We have come together in the presence of God, to witness the marriage of N. and N., to ask his blessing on them, and to share in their joy. Our Lord Jesus Christ was himself a guest at a wedding in Cana of Galilee, and through his Spirit he is with us now. 6

While your friends are seated at the beginning of the service, the priest will read The Preface. It reminds everybody present of some of the significant reasons for having a church wedding. The first sentence stresses the threefold dimension of the occasion.

(i) "*The presence of God*". We have come especially to 'his' house for the occasion.

(ii) *The witnesses* represent the human society, for life can never be lived privately and our marriage is bound to involve our families and friends.

(iii) The third dimension is of course you, *the bride and groom*.

Next we go on to think of Jesus. He went to a wedding and brought richness and new life to the occasion. Thus you invite him to yours and ask the same for yourselves. Sometime before your marriage, read in your Bible,

> ***"...there was a wedding at Cana in Galilee. The mother of Jesus was there, and Jesus and his disciples were guests also."***
>
> *John 2, v.1*

The Scriptures teach us that marriage is a gift of God in creation and a means of his grace, a holy mystery in which man and woman become one flesh. It is God's purpose that, as husband and wife give themselves to each other in love throughout their lives, they shall be united in that love as Christ is united with his Church.

The christian man and woman use the Bible to give them directions like sign posts on a journey. Marriage, we say, like so many of the lovely things in the world is a 'gift of God'. It is not something you work for and buy, not something you deserve by your effort, not something you take by strength of will or body, not even good luck that you found each other. For Christians, marriage is a 'gift'. See your partner as part of the loveliness of beauty of God's living creation which he offers and gives to you to care for and to love.

Underlying the passage beginning 'The Scriptures teach us' is that expressive story of Adam and Eve which puts into words and creates in the imagination what human couples, truly in love, find over and over again. Most of us accept today, that biologically we have developed our humanity and our sexuality from primitive forms of life. The Garden of Eden and the tale of Adam and Eve expresses not so much what life was like at the beginning, but what it is like now for those truly in love. God 'brought' her unto the man and Adam said ...

> ***"This is now bone of my bones, and flesh of my flesh ... Therefore shall a man leave his father and his mother and shall cleave unto his wife and they shall be one flesh".***
>
> *Genesis 2, v.23*

This is the experience of being 'in love'.

This strange expression 'one flesh' has meaning for many young people and develops and holds the two towards the maturity of a happy marriage — but not everybody finds it. Those who do, do well to remember it is a gift of God and it is difficult to explain in anything but poetic language. In Church we call it 'a mystery'. When Jesus was asked a difficult question on marriage, he referred his hearers back to what the scriptures said in Genesis. This is God's way, but we shall return to this later on.

The paragraph ends with the expressed desire that the couple shall be united as Jesus Christ is united with his living Church on earth. Today this is a reminder of those words in the Bible ...

> ***"Christ also loved The Church and gave himself for it — so ought men to love their wives — nourish and cherish them as The Lord does His Church".*** *Ephesians 5 v.29*

So as God gives us his creation, and as we know Jesus gave his life on the Cross, so a true marriage begins with the couple who 'give themselves to each other in love' and so receive a gift of God.

Three Good Reasons

Some people today don't bother to get married, they just live together. The Marriage Service explains that this is wrong and gives three reasons why people should solemnly make a marriage. Each reason begins with the same formula 'Marriage is given that ...' and we may summarise the reasons as follows:

It is given that they may enjoy

(a) Human completion and companionship.
(b) Sexual fulfilment of the body and the mind.
(c) The joy of children and a family.

(a) **Human completion and companionship**

Marriage is given, that husband and wife may comfort and help each other, living faithfully together in need and in plenty, in sorrow and in joy.

In days gone by women often spent nearly all of their adult lives in carrying, giving birth and suckling small children. At the beginning of this century the average length of a woman's life was 47 years, and of course when the old service was written it was very much less than that. The vital hope of many a couple getting married then was that children would be born and safely reared and would live to carry on the family trade or tend the farm. Thus in the old Marriage Service you will see that the 'increase of mankind' was the first thing mentioned. In the new service you will find the first thing mentioned is that 'husband and wife may comfort and help each other ...' because this seems to be uppermost in young couples' thoughts these days. When we say this we don't only have in mind the cooking and the washing up but rather the plumbing of the depths of what is called the human 'aloneness'. So much healthy development of the human adult depends on 'the blissful certainty of being wanted'. This is sound Christian psychology. Two people with different personalities, needs, fears and anxieties strive to establish this identity. Marriage offers a journey of mutual discovery which, at times, shows the depth of inadequacy and failure. The courage and trust of the partnership helps the fullness of the personality to develop.

(b) **Sexual fulfillment of the body and mind**

It is given, that with delight and tenderness they may know each other in love, and, through the joy of their bodily union, may strengthen the union of their hearts and lives.

For too long, the Church has given a negative lead to the understanding of sexuality. Very often it has said nothing. Worse it has sometimes suggested that sexual intercourse in marriage is good only for those who cannot live the life style of the monk or nun. Such a suggestion does occur in the old service. Today, the Church is anxious to redress the balance. It still believes that there is a proper and honoured place for celibacy and that many will fulfill themselves best by living single lives, but it also believes that for most of us, the joy and development of sexual unity is one of God's greatest gifts. Sexual experiences in true marriage will be a 'delight' to both. The Priest will speak in the new Service of you 'knowing each other' because in the Bible we read ...

> ***"Adam knew his wife and she conceived ..."***
> *Genesis 4, v. 1*

We may think we 'know' all sorts of things and people, but the husband and wife in physical intercourse open the way to a deeper 'knowing' and in this constant expression of love, find a joy which holds hearts close, and binds two often separate and quite divergent lives.

(c) **The joy of children and family**

It is given, that they may have children and be blessed in caring for them and bringing them up in accordance with God's will, to his praise and glory.

It is often assumed by young couples who come to be married in Church that 'nature' will keep them together. It is natural for some animals and birds to mate and stay together. We would be very short-sighted if we thought all humans 'naturally' stay together. If we look at the world wide human cultures, at the old Hindu custom of India, or primitive tribes of Africa or South America there are only a few signs of monogamy as it is called. In the Old Testament of the Bible, we read that the Hebrews likewise had very different customs from ours. Did not Solomon 'love many strange women'?

> ***"He had seven hundred wives, princesses, and three hundred concubines".*** *1 Kings 11, v. 3*

Jesus taught us to think back to God's creation and to see that God's way for us is a perpetual and permanent sexual relationship. This does not necessarily come 'naturally', it has to be seen and recognised and then worked at intentionally and purposefully. His critics would have had it otherwise; Jesus answered them

> ***"but in the beginning at the Creation, God made them male and female... and the two shall become one flesh. What God has joined together, man must not separate."*** *Mark 10, v. 6*

We see then, although children can be born of any or no true relationship, the Christian pattern is that they are born in love. Husband and wife bind themselves to enable the young to have that male and female care and protection which we believe is God's will in creation, and thus may grow up to live and grow to his 'praise and glory'.

The priest says to the congregation

But first I am required to ask anyone present who knows a reason why these persons may not lawfully marry, to declare it now. 7

The priest says to the couple

The vows you are about to take are to be made in the name of God, who is judge of all and who knows all the secrets of our hearts: therefore if either of you knows a reason why you may not lawfully marry, you must declare it now. 8

In days long gone it was possible to rush off to a priest who had an authority to marry and get married in haste in the dead of night! The present laws, which often seem horribly mundane and constricting to couples — not before banns are called; not after 6 p.m.; not in this place or that nice garden — are rules which try to make sure that the desire of youth to run away does not get its chance, for, whether we like it or not, when we marry two families become involved. A marriage inevitably effects a host of people, to think otherwise is to be purely selfish. We make a public presentation of the ring and the congregation behind you are there to witness, but also to pray for you. They are given a last chance to lodge a legal objection. The Priest likewise warns you that a true Christian marriage can only be performed when it is according to God's law. Should the law be infringed the marriage may indeed be declared null and void.

The Vows

The priest says to the bridegroom

N., will you take N. to be your wife? Will you love her, comfort her, honour and protect her, and, forsaking all others, be faithful to her as long as you both shall live? 9

He answers

I will.

The priest says to the bride

10 **N. will you take N. to be your husband? Will you love him, comfort him, honour and protect him, and, forsaking all others, be faithful to him as long as you both shall live?**

She answers

I will.

Engagements nowadays tend to be almost private affairs. Long ago the first question 'John will you take Jane to be your wife ...' and the complimentary question to 'Jane ...' belonged to the public engagement ceremony. It may seem silly to ask the question *now* for obviously Jane wouldn't be standing there if she was going to answer the question 'Will you take ...' 'No I won't'. What it does still do, is to show to all, your willing free consent to proceed.

The Bride's hand is, by custom, given by her father to the Priest. The actions in a marriage are just as important as the words. The father, with other members of the family, loved and looked after the Bride since she was a child, to them a gift of God. Now the Priest gives her hand, a gift of God, into the hand of her chosen husband. (There are sometimes circumstances where the father cannot or ought not to be the person to fulfill this gesture. In such cases it may be a brother, mother or uncle or even a friend. I have known instances when the Bride was truly alone due to family bereavements, and in such circumstances or other circumstances she may dispense with this sign which is now optional.) Some have felt the passing of the Bride's hand to be a relic from days when women were possessions to be disposed of. Most Brides find the custom of walking with father to church an affectionate support which they welcome on such a momentous occasion. Any Bride who simply prefers to offer her own hand is free to do so in the new Service.

The priest may receive the bride from the hands of her father.
The bride and bridegroom face each other.
The bridegroom takes the bride's right hand in his and says

Vows "A"

I, N., take you, N.., 11
to be my wife,
to have and to hold
from this day forward;
for better, for worse,
for richer, for poorer,
in sickness and in health,
to love and to cherish,
till death us do part,
according to God's holy law;
and this is my solemn vow.

They loose hands.
The bride takes the bridegroom's right hand in hers, and says

I, N., take you N.,
to be my husband,
to have and to hold
from this day forward;
for better, for worse,
for richer, for poorer,
in sickness and in health,
to love and to cherish,
till death us do part,
according to God's holy law;
and this is my solemn vow.

They loose hands.

Face to face. A direction has now appeared in the service that the couple face each other. It is left to each individual couple as to how they interpret 'to face'. What is important is that you remember that you are taking the promise to Jane or John as well as to God. It is a good thing therefore to look towards the Bride and vice versa as you take your vows. You may if you choose, decide to read your vows out of a book, not repeating them as is customary. The old custom of repetition dates from days when few could read. If vows are read casually, they lose so much sensitivity. The old way of repetition still suits most of us very well.

Which vows? When the new Service was being prepared it was known that all over the country there were people with such strong views on the nature of sexuality that if only one form of vows was provided, large numbers of folk would never use the new Service. Now you may take your vows in either form A or B (see pp. 11 & 27).

The difference is simply that in Vows B the obligations of husband to wife or wife to husband are slightly different. The man says 'to love, cherish and worship', the woman says 'to love, cherish and obey'.

Those who use Vows A will be those who specially want to stress the equality of the couple, who think that in these modern days anything else is quite wrong from a Christian standpoint. They, as a couple, will want to explore the ways in which they will best compliment one another according to their respective contributions, without suggesting at the outset how this may be done.

Those who use Vows B will be those who believe that sexually we are made very different in body and mind, and so we accept each other differently. It is important fully to understand what is meant by the words 'obey' and 'worship'. Obey does not mean 'do as you are told' in the normal English usage and you will find a full discussion about these important words in the Vows at the back of this book on page 25.

The meaning of the vows. Here, indeed, is the very essence of a Christian wedding. Here is the moment when your marriage in Church will be so different from the legal alliance you might have made in a Registry Office.

John says he will have and hold you

"from this day forward for better, for worse, for richer, for poorer."

You know, unless you live in the clouds, that there will be many times 'for worse'. A parish priest often spends more time helping marriages along in the 'worse' stages than he spends preparing the likes of yourselves at the beginning. The Christian couple see a marriage as an organic growing and living thing, like a tree. It may have to have branches lopped off here and there; it may have periods of drought; it may even grow up perpetually crooked but it lives through better or worse, through richer and poorer. Together, a couple create and live a marriage. No tree is a perfect tree, but some are very beautiful and some are very strong. Then you say

"in sickness and in health"

— you both may feel on top of the world now — a quick look at your families and their friends will show you it may not always be so. Somebody loves you enough to say, whatever may happen to you, I'll be there

"to love and cherish till death us do part"
He says he will love you according to God's holy law, that is to say, for ever, and only you, and then he makes this his solemn vow.

Now just what do you do 'to cherish' him? This lovely old English word means keep him warm! So this may mean give him a cocoa or a rum before going to bed; it may mean don't grab the blanket so that his side pulls out, it does mean that where there is warmth, there is life and love.

The woman's equality and freedom. As soon as the Groom finishes his vow, he loosens his hand and lowers it. The Bride then stretches out to take his hand (always the right hand in law). The significance of this is to stress the woman's freedom as a Christian. She freely and equally takes the decision of her own will.

The priest receives the ring(s). He says

Heavenly Father, by your blessing, let this ring be to N. and N. a symbol of unending love and faithfulness, to remind them of the vow and covenant which they have made this day; through Jesus Christ our Lord. Amen. 13

The bridegroom places the ring on the fourth finger of the bride's left hand, and holding it there, says

I give you this ring 14
as a sign of our marriage.
With my body I honour you,
all that I am I give to you,
and all that I have I share with you,
within the love of God,
Father, Son, and Holy Spirit.

If only one ring is used, before they loose hands the bride says

I receive this ring 15
as a sign of our marriage.
With my body I honour you,
all that I am I give to you,
and all that I have I share with you,
within the love of God,
Father, Son, and Holy Spirit.

The priest addresses the people

17 **In the presence of God, and before this congregation, N., and N., have given their consent and made their marriage vows to each other. They have declared their marriage by the joining of hands and by the giving and receiving of a ring. I therefore proclaim that they are husband and wife.**

The priest joins their right hands together and says

18 **That which God has joined together, let not man divide.**

The ring. The wedding ring (usually passed to the Priest by the Best Man) is in the form of an unbroken circle, which has no junction or end and is symbolic of the promise, just made, of unending love. It is given and received as a token of the pledge. The gold or wealth in the ring originally signified the husband's willingness to give his worldly goods to his bride and thus provide for her. The words now used with the ring by both John and Jane recall the preface read at the beginning of the Marriage Service:

(i) He/she will honour with the full physical and sexual love of the body;

(ii) he/she will give of the whole being of the person;

(iii) he/she will share all possessions

and this rounds off with a telling ascription

"within the love of God, Father, Son, and Holy Spirit."

The Christian who assented to belief in Father, Son and Holy Spirit at the font in Holy Baptism now says, all that I give today and promise today is part of God's love.

In the old Prayer Book service the man says to the woman "with all my worldly goods I thee endow". Since the Married Woman's Property Act, 1888 and the Matrimonial Homes Act, 1967, women have had property rights of their own and in legal litigation in times of matrimonial dispute every attempt is made to treat husband and wife as equals in property matters. Thus you will notice in the new Service both say to each other 'all that I have I share with you'.

A ring or rings? Provision has now officially been made in the new Service for those couples who may wish to adopt the custom of giving each other rings on their wedding day. The bride may offer the groom a ring to be put on with a similar promise. When the custom of a single ring being given or received is followed, the bride now accepts it making an identical affirmation. (In the old Service she accepts it silently.)

The Proclamation. The Couple are married by virtue of taking the vows and giving and accepting the ring. The Priest again joins their hands (he may also bind them with his stole) and declares solemnly, the words of Jesus

"That which God has joined together, let not man divide"
Mark 10, v. 9

It is important to say something about this proclamation because for so long we have been familiar with the phrase from the old Service

"Those whom God hath joined together let no man put asunder"

These old words sound superb, but it is not a correct translation of what Jesus said. There is no need here to tell you how this mistake arose. You will want to know what is wrong with it? 'Let no man' is singular and gives the impression that the Priest is looking at the people and warning them that nobody present, man or woman, should be guilty of upsetting (putting asunder) you two. Jesus, however, was answering a question as to whether the custom was right that allowed the male the privilege of writing a divorce note when he was tired of his wife's nagging, or burning the dinner. Jesus is saying, God created this marriage bond for us, it is not for mankind to undo it.

The congregation remain standing.
The husband and wife kneel, and the priest blesses them.

God the Father, **19**
God the Son,
God the Holy Spirit,
bless, preserve, and keep you;
the Lord mercifully grant you the riches of his grace,
that you may please him both in body and soul,
and, living together in faith and love,
may receive the blessings of eternal life. Amen.

The Blessing. Only you two are on your knees for this blessing, everybody else stands and prays over you and for you. It is very brief as you humbly seek a blessing as a seal on your words and actions.

The great solemnity of the priest calling on Father, Son and Holy Spirit should not be dismissed in your mind as an idle formula. In the

Church in medieval times, the priest said 'God the Father bless you, God the Son keep you, God the Holy Spirit lighten your understanding'; this has now become 'God the Father, God the Son, God the Holy Spirit, bless, preserve and keep you'. Old English castles have 'keeps', the safest and most secure spot, thus 'keep' means, may you be protected from spiritual danger. 'Preserve' in the kitchen implies that impurities have been disposed of and the contents will last, e.g. marmalade. The meaning is much the same here.

'The riches of His grace', by this time the couple have usually received quite a number of their presents, they are often abundantly blessed through other people parting with their 'riches'. Here 'the riches of His grace' mean the gifts of the Holy Spirit.

> ***"The harvest of the Spirit is love, joy, peace, patience, kindness, goodness, fidelity, gentleness and self-control"***
>
> *Galations 5, v. 22*

You will need these gifts in your married life as well as the new set of cutlery or Aunt Polly's bath towels. The Blessing continues that you may please God both in 'body and soul' — God really does care how you treat each other in bed, as well as how you say your prayers. Then live together 'in faith and love' and prepare each other for when 'death do us part', and you receive 'the blessing of eternal life'.

These acclamations may be used.

20 *Priest* **Blessed are you, heavenly Father;**
All **You give joy to bridegroom and bride.**

Priest **Blessed are you, Lord Jesus Christ:**
All **You have brought new life to mankind.**

Priest **Blessed are you, Holy Spirit of God;**
All **You bring us together in love.**

Priest **Blessed be Father, Son, and Holy Spirit:**
All **One God, to be praised for ever. Amen.**

The congregation will probably enjoy adding the Trinitarian acclamations 'Blessed are you heavenly Father' to the Priest's blessing. They have been silent for a very long time and they may be moved to want to say more now, than just an AMEN. If you have a good choir, there is no reason why they alone should not burst out with these acclamations for you if you so wish. It is printed, as it is, for the convenience of the normal, small congregation.

The Lesson and the Sermon

One of the main differences between the new Service and the old is the provision for a Lesson to be read. In the old Service a sermon was to be preached after the final blessing or if not, then an extensive series of quotations from the scriptures was ordered to be read. Now, the couple with the priest have the opportunity to choose their own Lesson (and the priest may or may not decide to preach). This is a magnificent opportunity for the couple to give the service a very personal character. You will do well to spend time together thinking this over. It may be your favourite passage of scripture or something particularly appropriate for a wedding. It must be from the Bible and the priest must, obviously, agree that it is suitable. On page 22 you will find a list of the Lessons suggested. It may be possible for you to ask for a particular friend or the Best Man or bridesmaid to read it, but first be certain that such a person is used to reading the scriptures in public and would be welcomed by the Priest to do it. You may, if you wish, sit down for the reading and address.

Together at the Altar

The first steps husband and wife take together are forward towards the Altar (if the design of the Church so allows, if not you remain where you are). In olden times the couple invariably received the Holy Communion on their wedding day, their first steps being towards the Lord's Table and then home to their own table for 'wedding breakfast' — it was for all in those days a real breaking of fast. You will walk together truly 'coupled' for the first time. At the Table you will be especially conscious of the risen presence of Christ Jesus at your wedding and you may also sense that you are presenting each other to him before you go anywhere else. There will be time now for deeper prayer and your own prayers. The first thing you have done in your new married life is to have walked together to 'His' table. It may be that in your subsequent married life you may try to remember His Day (Sunday) and put 'Him' first in your priorities of time and duties.

You may not want to walk up there in silence so you have a choice of psalm or another hymn which will be sung as you go hand in hand. (see page 21).

The Prayers

Kneel
The husband and wife kneel before the holy table.

24 *Priest* **Almighty God,**
you send your Holy Spirit
to be the life and light of all your people.
Open the hearts of these your children
to the riches of his grace,
that they may bring forth the fruit of the Spirit
in love and joy and peace;
through Jesus Christ our Lord, Amen.

26 *Priest* **Heavenly Father,**
maker of all things,
you enable us to share in your work of creation.
Bless this couple in the gift and care of children,
that their home may be a place of love,
security, and truth,
and their children grow up
to know and love you in your Son
Jesus Christ our Lord. Amen.

(a) The prayer of the heart

There is a bad custom of drawing hearts, cupids and arrows on trees. The heart is in our tradition, the centre of the emotions, the innermost part of 'me'. The first prayer dwells upon our hearts that they may not be rigid and hard but opened to the life of the Holy Spirit of God, day by day and year by year; that 'the riches' of the spirit may be given to you — "In love and joy and peace".

(b) The prayer for a family

Normally, when a young couple are married, the second prayer for a family will always be said. We turn from 'fruit of the spirit' to 'fruit of the body' — the children. Having children ought not to be a selfish decision but seen as a sharing in God's creative love. We ask that you may have a family, and that when you do, the children may find your home a place of 'love, security and truth'. (An alternative is provided for occasions when this prayer may be unsuitable.)

(c) **Prayers of your choice**

You may ask to have added in here prayers of your own choice. One or two will be quite sufficient. You may select them from the 'additional prayers' which are suggested in the service; (Pages 298–299) you may choose a prayer which you especially love; you may together write a prayer, and ask for it to be used; you may suggest a silence for private contemplation. (In this matter of choice, as in all others, your Priest will have experience and guidance to offer you). He will conclude by asking all your friends and family to join with you in the Lord's Prayer, which may be said in either the new or old form of words. Finally he gives a Blessing. This time it is not only for you, but for your parents, who will have their own wedding day much in mind, for your Best Man and bridesmaids, family and friends.

The priest blesses the couple and the congregation, saying

God the Holy Trinity make you strong in faith and love, defend 30
you on every side, and guide you in truth and peace; and the blessing of God Almighty, the Father, the Son, and the Holy Spirit, be among you and remain with you always. Amen.

Now Other Things to be Decided

Psalms and Hymns?

The Psalms were the songs of the Jews when Our Lord Himself went to prayer at the Temple and they have been used by Christians ever since with special reverence. You may choose one of the three printed in the Alternative Service Book for marriage or a favourite of your own, or if you wish you may have no psalm at all. (See pages 294 and 295 of the Alternative Service Book).

Psalm 67

Congregational joy is the theme. It begins by asking for a blessing. It asks if you will, in your married life, give praise and place to God, then it adds, the earth yields its fruitfulness.

Psalm 121

This is a psalm about going on a journey. God will watch you do not stumble during the day or get harmed while you sleep. You will both be beginning together the greatest journey of your lives.

Psalm 128

This psalm is especially for weddings. The first two verses are directed to the man that he should honour God, and enjoy the results of his work. The next two verses dwell on the woman, her home and family. It ends with the hope

(i) that you will have some worldly prosperity
(ii) that you will live to see your grandchildren, and
(iii) that your nation may enjoy peace.

The Hymns

Two may well be sufficient. A hymn is essentially a chorus activity of praise, one in which you want everybody to feel they have a part. It is no good choosing fine words for a wedding but then having a tune nobody will sing. It is often best to choose two good well known hymns which have a ring of joy about them, but which may have nothing specifically to do with marriage. Read the words carefully, 'Fight the good fight' for example can take on an unintended significance. These are popular, but choose something different, more personal of your own if you can.

Christ is made the sure Foundation
Come down, O Love Divine
Crown with love, Lord this glad day
Father, Lord of all creation
For the beauty of the earth
God of mercy, God of grace
Gracious spirit, Holy Ghost
Guide me, O thou great Redeemer
Immortal, invisible, God only wise
Jesus, Lord we pray
King of glory, King of peace
Lead us, Heavenly Father, lead us
Let all the world in every corner sing
Lord of all hopefulness, Lord of all joy
Love divine, all loves excelling
Morning has broken
Now thank we all our God
O perfect Love, all human thought transcending
O praise ye the Lord! praise Him in the height
O Thou who gavest power to love
Praise, my soul, the King of Heaven
Praise to the Lord, the Almighty, the King of creation
The Lord's my Shepherd, I'll not want

Choosing the Reading?

The suggestions made in the Service are tabulated here for your convenience. However, you are not bound by them and may choose anything you particularly desire from the Bible if it has the goodwill of the priest taking your service.

Genesis 1, 26 – 28, 31	The Creation
Matthew 7, 21, 24 – 27	Firm foundation
Mark 10, 6 – 9	What God has joined
John 2, 1 – 11	The wedding at Cana in Galilee
John 15, 9 – 12	Love one another
Romans 12, 1 – 2, 9 – 13	Offering and dedication
1 Corinthians, 13	Faith, hope and love
Ephesians 3, 14 – 21	Christ dwell in your hearts
Ephesians 5, 21 – 33	Duties of wives and husbands
Colossians 3, 12 – 17	Giving thanks
1 John 4, 7 – 12	God is love

The Order of Service?

One of the most important changes made in the new Marriage Service is to allow our Parish Churches some opportunity of varying the order of service. Vicars, organists and choirs will, undoubtedly come to decide what suits a particular Church best and will not be wanting to chop and change the local order used for every couple.

The chief structural decision that has to be taken is whether or not the lesson (and the sermon) should come before you take your vows or afterwards. Do you want the Readings from Scriptures and the Sermon to give you guidance before you make your own vows of Holy Matrimony or do you want these things to be an encouragement and guidance after you have taken your vows?

In the old Prayer Book the order was, roughly speaking:

The Preface
The Vows
Procession to the Holy Table
Prayers
Sermon

Now it may be one or other of the following:

The Preface	OR	The Lesson (and Sermon)
The Vows		The Preface
The Lesson (and Sermon)		The Vows
Procession to the Holy Table		Procession to the Holy Table
The Prayers		The Prayers

If it is thought to be rather blunt to begin either service in this way and that a response from the congregation and a prayer to the Lord is the proper way to begin, the sections printed at the very beginning may be included, see page 287, the Alternative Service Book.

The Holy Communion

In medieval times it was the normal and natural thing for the couple to receive the Sacrament of the Holy Communion on their wedding day. In the last three hundred years, for various reasons which we do not need to go into now, the 'usual' wedding has followed the Book of Common Prayer Service to the end but little notice was taken of the final rubric which read:

"It is convenient" (i.e. it is suggested) "that the new-married persons should receive the Holy Communion at the time of their Marriage, or at the first opportunity after their Marriage."

Despite this rubric the great majority of weddings solemnised in the twentieth century in the Church of England have been without Communion, and when guests have turned up and found themselves led on from the marriage vows into Holy Communion they have been surprised. They may have thought it High Church because many weddings in the Roman Catholic Church continued to have Nuptial Mass. In the last twenty years a Communion has become much more common and is certainly more and more requested. It is a natural and normal request today when both you and your fiancé are communicants in your own churches.

Those of you who are confirmed and communicants will know that in the Holy Communion Service we find an especially close and intimate relationship with Our Lord. It is a mystery very hard to put into words. It is something one wants to do at moments in life of great significance or great joy. It is, however, much easier now to include a communion in a wedding because the new Services allow a great deal of abbreviation and if you choose to make it so, the Marriage Service with Holy Communion may last not more than ten minutes longer than a service without a communion.

The Collect, Epistle and Gospel may be used either before your Marriage Vows and be part of the introduction or they may be used later in place of the ordinary lesson. At the Altar prior to the marriage prayers, the service may proceed with the Eucharistic Thanksgiving Prayer and then immediately comes the receiving of the Sacrament. Parts of the normal Communion service, e.g. the confession, and the prayers for others customary on a Sunday may be omitted on your wedding day. Your Vicar will show you how this is done. (cf page 301 The Alternative Service Book). If you look at that page it may make you think your service is going to be terribly long. Do remember, 'optional parts of the services may be omitted'.

Two questions still remain. Should the Communion include just the Priest and the new Husband and Wife or should it include as many of the congregation who may wish to join you? I have known both work quite successfully. I have also known the Bride and Groom ask in advance the Parents or just the Bridesmaids and the Best Man to join them in Holy Communion. This will all depend on your family circumstances. Very often one side of the family would feel differently about it than the other, in which case it is better that it should be just you two. Time is another factor; it is important that the service should be of an acceptable length, not only for you but also for your guests. Whichever way you plan it you should, yourselves, remain kneeling in the centre before the Altar as others come around you.

One final word. Suppose you do not both happen to be Church of England, what then? One of the new Canons (Laws) of the Church of England (B15A) allows those who are communicants in other Churches to make their Communion when visitors to the Church of England. If, for example, your fiancé is a regular Methodist or Roman Catholic communicant, the Church of England will not refuse you a communion service. Again talk to your Vicar about this.

Vows A or Vows B?

In England since 1549, the word 'obey' has been part of the marriage vow. In 1928 when a new Prayer Book was proposed it was felt that the word 'obey' might be optional, so for the last half century although the marriage service was not changed by Parliament, there has been a continual dilemma as to whether or not the word "obey" ought to be used. The theologians are as deeply divided about it as ever but, now for the first time, Bride and Groom may genuinely decide for themselves.

As I said on page 12 those who use vows B will be those who believe that our sexuality makes us different from one another, male and female, and in marriage we will want to express this. It has nothing to do with status or seniority; it has to do with the way one relates to the other. Those who accept vows B will say their vow is rooted in scriptures whilst those who use vows A will say that those scriptures were fashioned according to the subordinate position of women in past ages and are not really relevant now.

Let us see then what the scriptures say in the *New English Bible:*

> ***"Wives be subject to your husbands as to the Lord; for the man is the head of the woman, just as Christ also is the head of the Church."***
> *Ephesians 5, v. 22*

Having been to school where we had Headmasters, Head Teachers or Head Girls, we immediately think that "head" means the 'boss'. Not so if we look back to what this writer was saying earlier:

"So shall we fully grow up into Christ. He is the head, and on him the whole body depends. Bonded and knit together by every constituent joint, the whole frame grows together ..."
Ephesians 4, v. 15

The writer likens the Church of God on earth to a human body with legs, arms, ears and eyes and just as the brain in the head functions through all the nerves and limbs of the body, so does Jesus need us all to fulfill his will on earth. Thus the husband will need his wife in a living, organic, close relationship, but one where the function of the one is not necessarily the function of the other.

You will notice the phrase "Wives be subject to your husbands"; similar phrases occur several times in the Bible. St. Paul says

"Wives be subject to your husbands: that is your Christian duty unto your own husbands as it is fit in the Lord"
Colossians 3, v. 18

St. Peter says

"In the same way you women must accept the authority of your husbands, so that if there are any of them who disbelieve the Gospel they may be won over, without a word being said by observing the chaste and reverent behaviour of their wives" *1 Peter 3, v. 1*

Each time the word used is submit, or be subject to, or accept the authority of — never 'obey'. Neither the Authorised Version, the Revised Standard Version nor the New English Bible ever uses the word 'obey' to translate what is intended. The Greek word for 'obey' is, however, used elsewhere, e.g.

"Children obey your parents" *Colossians 3, v. 19*

The Bible never tells wives to 'obey' in the normal English use of that word but it does tell them to:

"reverence her husband" *Authorised Version Ephesians 5, v. 3*
"respect her husband" *Revised Standard Version Ephesians 5, v. 3*
"pay her husband all respect" *New English Bible Ephesians 5, v. 3*

The function then of 'obey' in the Marriage Service is not one of slavery or blind acceptance of authority, but the acceptance of what some find to be a natural leadership, remembering that leadership in Christian terms always indicates a service given, not a submission required.

Why then did the revisers of the Marriage Service not use another word for 'obey'? Simply because an alternative couldn't be found that would command general agreement. 'Respect' was suggested but again we speak of children respecting their parents, so little was to be gained by such a change.

Before 1549 in a still older English use the bride promised to take her wedded husband

> ***"To have and to hold from this day for better, for worse, for richer, for poorer, in sickness and in health, to be bonour and buxom in bed and at bort till death ..."***

There was no obey then! 'At bort' meant at board, at the table. 'Bonour' is associated with bonny, bonnaire, meaning gentle. 'Buxom' was then a modern use of the word 'boughsome' which meant like a bough of a tree, bending not rigid, but buxom gradually changed in meaning, to be used of another characteristic female attribute, so that won't do today either!

In the vows of the old Service there was no balance for the word "obey" in the vow of the Groom, but when giving the ring he said:

> ***"with my body I thee worship".***

The word chosen to balance the 'obey' in vows "B" is thus the verb to 'worship', because this was the word used in the old service of the husband to his wife. It does not mean bow down and adore. We use the word of going to Church to worship — to give God his worth. We use it of our Mayor 'Your worship' — a person of worth. We men use it of the lady whom we choose to marry in love for she is worth so much to us.

Vows "B" 12

I, N, take you, N,
to be my wife,
to have and to hold
from this day forward;
for better, for worse,
for richer, for poorer,
in sickness and in health,
to love, cherish, and worship,
till death us do part,
according to God's holy law;
and this is my solemn vow.

I, N, take you N,
to be my husband,
to have and to hold
from this day forward;
for better, for worse,
for richer, for poorer,
in sickness and in health,
to love, cherish, and obey,
till death us do part,
according to God's holy law;
and this is my solemn vow.

Signing the Register?

Most Churches put out the Register in the vestry and the couple go there to sign after the final Blessing of congregation. Alternative provision is made, however, for the Register to be signed immediately after the Blessing of the couple midway in the Service. There are good arguments in favour of both customs.

It is important to remember that sixteen signatures may be required. This does take time and care. It is very important that unnecessary persons do not come into the vestry and cause pointless delay; nobody wants to wait upwards of fifteen minutes for you to reappear through the door! A photographer is often present and should be discouraged from asking for posed pictures. One photograph as the Bride signs is usually quite adequate. The Groom and the Bride sign their names in their usual manner in both registers; it is not necessary that they shall sign their names in full if they are not in the habit of doing so, but care must be taken that when initials are used they correspond, or at least do not disagree, with the full name written in column 2 of the Register. The Bride signs her maiden name. Both make three signatures. Two adult witnesses sign their signatures and the Priest adds his. Usually it is the Best Man and the Bride's father who are invited to sign as witnesses, but it may be a bridesmaid or any other adult you request. You take away with you a copy of the Registration. Should you later require an additional copy of the certificate this can usually be provided by the Vicar of the Parish where you were married but it involves additional legal fees for the work and time spent.

Finally, do look again at the Foreword at the beginning of this guide. The Archbishop's last words come appropriately here —

"May you be richly blessed in your life together."